UPDATED AND REVISED

A Guide to
Time Management Strategies
for Commanding Your Day

PAUL H. BURTON

DONE! 2.0
Updated and Revised

*A Guide to
Time Management Strategies
for Commanding Your Day*

Copyright © 2017 by Paul H. Burton

All rights reserved. No part of this book may be reproduced
or transmitted in any form or by any means, electronic or
mechanical, including photocopying, recording or by any
information storage and retrieval system without written
permission from the author, except for the inclusion of
quotations in a review.

Published by:
Paul H. Burton
www.quietspacing.com

Page layout by MiraBookSmart, Chesterfield, MO 63005

Printed in the United States of America

ISBN 978-1-9781305-1-7

About Paul H. Burton

Paul H. Burton is a former attorney, software executive, and successful entrepreneur. He helps clients gain command of their day, get more done, and enjoy greater personal and professional satisfaction. Paul is available for keynote presentations, interactive seminars, and individualized coaching services. You can learn more about Paul and his work at www.quietspacing.com.

Other Books by Paul H. Burton

— Available on Amazon

Done ... Again:
Ten New Ways to Make Better Use of Your Time

Wait:
Why You Procrastinate
& What You Can Do About It

Orchestrate:
Four Productivity Skills
Every Manager Needs

The Waterfall Effect:
Six Principles for Productive Leadership

Send:
A Dozen Ways to Make
Email Productive Again

Triage:
Rescuing Your Inbox

Table of Contents

	Page
Forward	1
Introduction	3
Challenges & Goals	5
Regaining Command of Your Email	7
Running Your Day More Productively	17
Task Completion Strategies	27
More Productive Workspaces	39
Conclusion	49

Forward

The original manuscript for this book was crafted in 2008. It, too, contained twenty-four suggestions for making the most of our time. Interestingly, some of the original recommendations still apply today, but many have changed.

What's changed most since the first writing of this book is the sense of urgency we feel to get things done and stay responsive to others. This urgency has continued to mount steadily year-over-year with no peak in sight. Now, more than ever, it's vitally important to make the most of the time we have.

To that end, this new edition will take even less time to consume than the last. The suggestions and their explanations have been streamlined to provide the reader a concise and cogent group of ideas on how to get more done while staying responsive to others.

The hope is that this topic – time management (a.k.a., productivity) – continues to be a focal effort for all professionals who want to lead rewarding personal and professional lives.

Introduction

We are bombarded by interruptions and distractions throughout the day. They hamper our ability to get things done. They interrupt our focused efforts and reduce our productivity. Getting more done each day occurs when the unnecessary interruptions and distractions are reduced.

For example, getting just six minutes more of work done each day results in twenty-four hours of additional productivity each year; that's three days of work off your desk each year...six minutes at a time.

The following chapters will focus on four topical areas. Each area will contain six suggestions, specific examples, and a smattering of client stories to help you understand the reasons behind each suggestion and how it can be applied. The goal here is to find one or two from the two dozen recommendations to start getting those six minutes back.

Challenges & Goals

Before jumping into the topical chapters, let's identify the challenges we face each day and the goals we have for being here. Please select the biggest productivity challenge you face and the most important goal you have for the program from the lists below.

Biggest Daily Challenge

- ☐ Interruptions
- ☐ Distractions
- ☐ Organizational
- ☐ Emergencies
- ☐ Stress
- ☐ Overwhelmed
- ☐ Prioritization

Most Important Goal

- ☐ Focus
- ☐ Command
- ☐ Balanced
- ☐ Directed
- ☐ Responsive
- ☐ Productive
- ☐ Effective

Regaining Command of Your Email

Quick Reference Chart

Fill in the Blanks

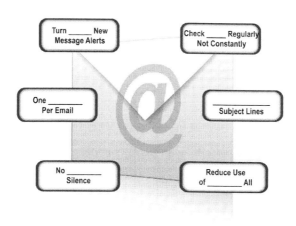

Email is the global *de facto* communication standard. Business use of email continues to grow. Email is also a hybrid form of communication—a written form used conversationally. This hybrid nature, coupled with habits developed early in its use, results in email being both the boon and the bane of the modern work world. It is the boon because we can communicate globally, twenty-four hours a day. It is the bane because everyone else can too!

Consider these suggestions to make email part of a more productive day.

1. Turn New Message Alerts Off

New message alerts were valuable when email was new. We only received five emails per day back then and needed to be alerted to their arrival.

Times have changed. Now, we receive five messages per minute. The new message alert serves only to distract us from other productive efforts, resulting in time lost getting back up to speed when we return to our efforts after checking the alert.

For example, it takes four seconds to look at a new email, determine its importance, and then act accordingly. If we receive 100 alerts a day, then we're losing four hundred seconds (6 minutes 40 seconds) each day just checking the 'ding'! That's well over twenty-four hours per year lost to this one activity.

2. Check Email Regularly Versus Constantly

Staying responsive to others while getting work done is a difficult balance. Regularly checking email versus constantly checking email is one way to achieve this balance. Staying focused on one thing—even for a short period of time—produces higher quality work faster. That's a positive result.

The frequency of inbox visits varies from day-to-day depending on other demands. However, a good rule of thumb is every fifteen minutes. That allows focused efforts and responsiveness to cohabitate.

Finally, when checking email, treat it like regular mail. Delete the trash, file the filing, and leave the rest in the inbox for future effort. Decluttering the inbox along the way makes finding and working on important messages easier to do.

3. Craft Single-Subject Emails

As a hybrid communication method, email has incorporated many conversational nuances. Not all of them are good or productive. One bad habit is switching topics mid-message. This is a normal conversational behavior, but it doesn't translate well to email—a written form.

Consider how physical letters were crafted: one subject in each letter. The reasons were simple. Not only did it focus the writer and reader on one subject—more effective—it was easier to file and to find.

These goals—effectiveness and ease of use—also pertain to emails. Thus, only discuss one subject in each email. If a new subject needs to be communicated to the same person, start a new email.

4. Leverage the Subject Line

Another bad email habit is the failure to craft good subject lines. The subject line is one of the few pieces of information every email recipient sees. Yet, most subject lines are only marginally communicative. Here are some examples of good and bad subject lines:

Bad Subject Line

- Question
- Meeting Tomorrow
- Need Information

Good Subject Line

- Question—Thompson Matter—Deadline=End of Business Today
- Meeting Tomorrow—Smith Matter—2:00 p.m. Eastern—Conf Rm 12 North
- Need Information—Robertson Deal—Deadline=Tuesday at Noon Eastern

The bad subject line emails tell the reader little, requiring the email to be opened and read before any meaningful action occurs. That's a waste of time. The good subject line emails tell the recipient what they need to know without ever opening the message. They're more effective and more efficient. Moreover, it is much easier to find and file the good subject line emails.

5. No Radio Silence

We have a strange relationship with email. We send and receive hundreds of emails each day. We work hard to stay on top of our work, and occasionally, we fail to keep others informed as to our progress. This is a bad habit because no news is always bad news to the person expecting to hear from us!

Make a habit of updating those with whom you work on a regular basis regarding your progress on the projects at hand. One good rule of thumb is to do these update emails at the end of each day as way to button up that day before going home.

6. Reduce Use of 'Reply All'

'Reply all' is often required to keep everyone in the loop and to document effort properly. However, it's not *always* required. One study found that people overuse 'reply all' about 20 percent of the time. If we all get one hundred emails a day (a low estimate) and we all reduce our use of 'reply all' by twenty percent, we'd all have twenty fewer emails per day that we didn't need to open, read, and delete. How many minutes would that save? All it takes is making one consideration: Does *everyone* on this email thread need my response?

Decide if any of the above suggestions make sense. If so, implement them and start getting those precious six minutes per day back!

Email Productivity Exercise – Pick a Winner

Take a moment to consider these six suggestions. Put a check mark next to the one you are willing to try today.

- ☐ Turn of New Message Alerts
- ☐ Check Email Regularly Versus Constantly
- ☐ Craft Single-Subject Emails
- ☐ Leverage the Subject Line
- ☐ No Radio Silence
- ☐ Reduce Use of 'Reply All'

Consider the following questions when making your choice. Feel free to use the provided space to write out your answers.

1. Why do you like this tip?
2. How does it impact you positively?
3. What steps will you take to implement it

Answers to Questions:

Running Your Day More Productively

Quick Reference Chart

Fill in the Blanks

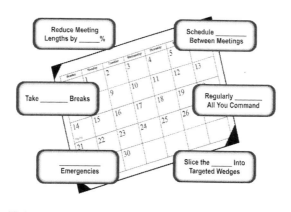

The workday is frenetic. It is filled with meetings, calls, assignments, and constant requests. Running a productive day requires a delicate touch to balance others' needs against work that must be done.

Consider these suggestions to remain productive throughout a busy day.

1. Reduce Meeting Lengths by Twenty-Five Percent

There are only two bad answers as to why one-hour meetings exist: One, that's the way it's always been done, or two, Outlook said so. Consider cutting all meetings by twenty-five percent. One-hour meetings drop to forty-five minutes, and thirty-minute meetings drop to twenty-five. Imagine how much more could be done with those extra minutes!

2. Schedule Time Between Meetings

Running from meeting to call to meeting to call is more than exhausting; it is ineffective. Much is lost in the transitions—good ideas, takeaways, prep time, etc. Carve a few minutes out between each appointment to debrief from the last appointment, prepare for the next one, or to check in with teammates. Do this by inserting a short "Unavailable" event on the calendar after every actual appointment. Many "Unavailables" will get lost, but the one or two that survive are invaluable.

3. Take Short Breaks

The mind is productivity's engine. It requires periods of rest in order to perform optimally. Find ways to take short breaks during the day to recharge the mind. Walk around the office floor or go grab some coffee; do anything that gives the mind a short rest. Then, jump back into the work. It is amazing how much gets done after even a five-minute break!

4. Regularly Survey All You Command

One key to staying on top of things is to periodically stop and take stock of what is happening.

Counterintuitively, slowing down can be faster. Taking a short break to match time availability with workload often results in doing more because this small planning effort better utilizes the time available to produce a work product.

A trap for the unwary is the morning habit of replying to overnight emails with answers like "Okay!" or "Got it, will do!" The reason these are dangerous is that they are acknowledgements of receipt **and** commitments to act. It's the latter—the commitment to act— that's dangerous because many of these emails have unclear deadlines such as "ASAP" or "Immediately," and we've just committed to that by responding with "Okay!" or "Got it, will do!"

The reality is that we all have existing commitments on our lists for today. Sending out morning responses just adds a few Johnny-come-latelys. When we arrive at the office, we'll most likely find we can't get everything done today. Now, we must decide whom to disappoint first! Not a great way to start the day.

An alternative is to acknowledge receipt without committing to the deadline. This is done by using a different response language, such as "This looks great, I'll come see you in an hour." or "Got it, I'll be in the office at 9:00 and will call you then." We've acknowledged receipt, thereby assuaging the sender's concern regarding whether we've seen the email. We've also taken command of the item, but we didn't commit to any built-in (and possibly unreasonable) deadlines. In fact, we bought a little time to get to the office and see what the day holds before we get back to the sender with a more realistic idea on what can get done by when.

5. Expect Emergencies

Optimism can undermine productivity. An 8-to-5 workday does *not* result in eight hours of time to work on what is already on our list. The exigent needs of each day fill much of that day's available time. So if we're committing to deadlines based on eight hours of available time to work and today's emergency takes three hours, that means we're three hours behind on our deadlines by day's end. Oh, and that makes tomorrow that much further behind too!

To remedy this situation, to the extent possible, plan for several hours of unscheduled time each day to deal with urgent matters that arise. Otherwise, the day's end only brings disappointment—the need to inform others that the work promised did not get done.

6. Slice the Day into Targeted Wedges

In fly fishing, there is the 10 & 2 casting rhythm. It means that the person casting the rod first cocks the rod back to the 10:00am position on the clock. (The caster's head represents 12:00pm.) Once there, the caster waits a moment for the fly line to catch up to the rod's action. Then, the caster thrusts the rod forward to the 2:00pm position on the clock and the fly line snaps forward and stretches out towards the targeted spot. The process and the rhythm is timed to produce a good cast.

Studies have found that most people have a natural productivity rhythm. We usually possess the greatest mental energy in the morning, less at mid-day, and the least towards the end of the day. What if we targeted our efforts into the wedges of the day best suited for the work that needs doing? Consider these wedges:

- <u>Morning – 8:00am to 11:00am</u>. Do the hard, individual effort tasks, the ones that take the most mental energy. Avoid scheduling meetings and calls during this period. Focus this wedge of time on doing.

- <u>Mid-Day – 11:00am to 2:00pm</u>. Do the collaborative work during the middle of the day. This is where meetings and phone calls are best scheduled. We can share our available energy among the participants.

- <u>Late Day – 2:00pm to 5:00pm</u>. Do the administrative work during this wedge, the items that must get done but require less energy to complete.

The times listed above are estimates and not everything can be scheduled into its best wedge. However, attempts to match the work with the available mental energy will produce a better overall result.

Grab one of these immediately actionable suggestions to make the best of the time available today!

Running Your Day Exercise – Pick a Winner

Take a moment to consider these six suggestions. Put a check mark next to the one you are willing to try today.

- ☐ Reduce Meeting Lengths by Twenty-Five Percent

- ☐ Schedule Time Between Meetings

- ☐ Take Short Breaks

- ☐ Leverage the Subject Line

- ☐ Regularly Survey All You Command

- ☐ Slice the Day into Targeted Wedges

Consider the following questions when making your choice. Feel free to use the provided space to write out your answers.

1. Why do you like this tip?
2. How does it impact you positively?
3. What steps will you take to implement it

Answers to Questions:

_____

_____

_____

_____

_____

_____

_____

_____

_____

_____

_____

_____

_____

_____

Task Completion Strategies

Multi-Tasking Exercise

Let's do a fun exercise before we move on to the strategies for getting more checked off the to-do list. You need some way to time yourself, such as the stopwatch function on your smartphone.

First Pass
The word "inefficient" is spelled out below. Two rows of eleven lines each are written below it.

Time yourself conducting the following activity. Remember, go as fast as you can so that we can take the least amount of time possible for the exercise.

Start by placing the "i" of "inefficient" on the first line on the first row. Then, place the number "1" on the first line of the second row. Then, put the letter "n" on the second line of the first row and the number "2" on the second line of the second row. Proceed up and down like this until you have completed spelling the word "inefficient" and writing the numbers one to eleven.

Record the time it takes you to complete this first pass of the exercise.

INEFFICIENT

— — — — — — — — — — —

— — — — — — — — — — —

Second Pass
"Inefficient" and the two rows of eleven lines appear a second time below. We're going to change one rule on the second pass of the exercise. Of course, this pass will also be timed.

This time instead of alternating between spelling and counting, time yourself writing the entire word out first across the top line and then writing the numbers one through eleven across the bottom line.

Record the time it takes you to complete the second pass.

INEFFICIENT

_ _ _ _ _ _ _ _ _

_ _ _ _ _ _ _ _ _

How did your times compare? Most people complete the first pass in about twenty-two seconds and the second pass in about thirteen seconds. The reason the second pass produces the same result as the first but 40 percent faster is because of something called a "**switch cost**."

The first pass required us to switch back and forth between spelling and counting. Each switch takes a moment of time. We must catch up to where we were on the last task prior to the switch before we can move forward again. Even in this short example, you can see that multitasking takes significantly more time to achieve the same result.

Switch costing also results in more mistakes. In this example, people often misspell the word. That's because spelling is a higher-order mental task, so people tend to misspell the word in the rush to "beat the clock."

This point of this simple example: Multi-tasking is inefficient.

Quick Reference Chart

Fill in the Blanks

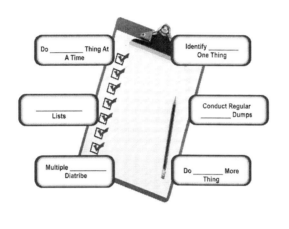

We need to find ways to manage the flow of work more efficiently now that we know multi-tasking isn't the best way to get things done. Here are some recommendations for smoothing out the daily work flow.

1. Do One Thing at a Time

Multi-tasking is neurologically impossible. The intellectually minded can read the Stanford University study that first broke the bad news: http://news.stanford.edu/news/2009/august24/multitask-research-study-082409.html. The brave can simply ride in a car where the driver is texting and driving!

Multi-tasking results in something called switch costing—the time it takes to switch back and forth between tasks. That "cost" adds up quickly, not to mention the amount of energy wasted and the level of stress experienced.

Focus is where productivity occurs. Seek ways to focus on one thing at a time. Turning off message alerts and establishing regular office hours—both discussed above—are good examples of creating quiet work environments that facilitate focus.

2. Identify Today's One Thing

Treading water, that is how many days feel. One way to combat that feeling and get more done is to pick one thing each day—just one—that *will* get done. Even checking only one thing off the list feels good. The work year consists of two hundred and forty days. Getting today's one thing done means that two hundred and forty "feel goods" occur each year. Not bad, huh?

3. Leverage Lists

Belle Beth Cooper, a *Fast Company* writer, said about list making: "We pack all the madness and ambiguity of life into a structured form of writing" ("The Surprising History of the To-Do List and How to Design One That Actually Works," *Buffer*, October 13, 2013, http://blog.bufferapp.com/the-origin-of-the-to-do-list-and-how-to-design-one-that-works). Lists allow us to create spatial relationships among our tasks, focus our attention on individual to-dos (versus their totality), and quiet our minds by getting everything committed to written form.

4. Conduct Regular Core Dumps

Where is the noisiest place on earth? It is right between the ears. All those thoughts are bouncing around at billions of bits per second. It's a wonder anything ever gets done! Conversely, the mind is the key tool in producing work. Quiet down that workspace by core dumping. Get everything out of there. Write it down. Add it to an app. Dictate it. Just get it out. The result is a quiet, focused mind that is very productive.

5. Multiple Monitors Diatribe

We began this section with an exercise that proves humans can't multi-task. So, what's with the multiple monitors? We now know we can't use them both at the same time. However, there are two things we can do with multiple monitors. First, they're useful when we're aggregating disparate information into a single document. For example, when we're pulling together information on a specific matter from different sources into a single summary document. That's a good use of multiple monitors.

Second, when we're not aggregating disparate data, the second thing we can do with multiple monitors is ***turn off*** the one(s) we're not using!

6. Do One More (Little) Thing

Before walking out the door each day, do one more (little) thing. File something. Return a call. Just make it something small and quick. Doing this will result in over two hundred more things getting done each year!

Which of these suggestions appeal to you? Put one or two of them into practice today and start getting those six minutes back!

Task Completion Exercise – Pick a Winner

Take a moment to consider these six suggestions. Put a check mark next to the one you are willing to try today.

- ☐ Do One Thing at a Time
- ☐ Identify Today's One Thing
- ☐ Leverage Lists
- ☐ Conduct Regular Core Dumps
- ☐ Multiple Monitors Diatribe
- ☐ Do One More (Little) Thing

Consider the following questions when making your choice. Feel free to use the provided space to write out your answers.

1. Why do you like this tip?
2. How does it impact you positively?
3. What steps will you take to implement it

Answers to Questions:

More Productive Workspaces

Quick Reference Chart

Fill in the Blanks

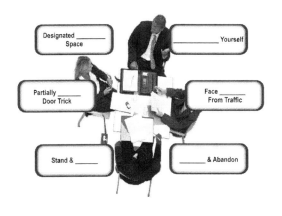

Where we work physically and how we work together in groups is a ripe source for small productivity changes that produce a lasting positive effect. Read the following six suggestions to determine which one or two of them you can incorporate into your day.

1. Create a Designated Workspace

Clear an area of everything. Place in that spot *one thing* to work on at a time. Having a designated workspace with only one thing in it eliminates the effects of peripheral vision.

Peripheral vision extends one hundred and twenty degrees in all directions. It's a survival mechanism and can't be turned off. Everything within that sphere is being "seen" by the brain, which causes mini-distractions. Achieve laser focus on the work at hand by clearing the viewfinder of all peripheral distractions.

Meet Jeff. Jeff has nice neat piles all over his desk. Some are six inches high and some are two feet high. The piles form a horseshoe around his desk, leaving him a small rectangle in the middle for him to work. I'm sure you've seen this desk before.

Jeff created a designated workspace on his desk by placing all the piles on the floor in front of his desk—out of his sight. Moving those piles out of Jeff's line of sight quieted down all the voices in his head reminding him about all the other work he needed to get done. That quieting allowed Jeff to focus on the one thing in front of him, resulting in better work done faster.

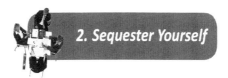

2. Sequester Yourself

One way to eliminate constant interruptions by others is to sequester yourself away in a quiet place, such as a conference or caucus room. Take one or two projects along with you, sit down and work on those tasks, and then get back to the fray. Sequestering for as little as thirty minutes greatly increases productivity on important work.

Abby was an up-and-comer at her work, so she was always very busy. She was also a single mother of a toddler in day care. She had to leave at 5:00 p.m. sharp to pick up her daughter. Abby used the sequestering suggestion to succeed at both.

Once or twice a day, Abby would sequester herself in a private place on her floor—door closed and one or two files of work with her. After a short period—thirty to forty-five minutes—Abby would return to her own workspace and get back into the fray. This gave her time to concentrate *and* time to collaborate throughout the day.

3. Partially Closed Door Trick

Drive-by interruptions are the enemy of productivity. These are not the necessary interruptions—when people come by physically or electronically for work purposes.

I'm all for office collegiately. I call it lunch!

Avoid these by *partially* closing the office door and setting specific times to meet with colleagues. The analogy is the college professor who maintains office hours for student questions.

4. Face Away from Traffic

Most offices are arranged with the occupant's chair facing the door. Peripheral vision negatively affects focus here as well. Traffic passes by the office door all day long and the instinctual response is to look up—another mini-distraction—or worse, if passersby stop and come into the office.

Spin the desk ninety degrees to the right or left so that it faces a wall. This arrangement eliminates the unnecessary interruptions caused by peripheral vision picking up passersby. Go one step further by ensuring the door is partially closed and behind one shoulder.

5. Stand & Stop

Sometimes you just can't avoid an *unnecessary* interruption. Once someone has distracted you, the only strategy is to minimize the interruption. That's where the Stand & Stop maneuver is helpful. When an *unnecessary* distractor comes into your workspace, immediately stand up. This communicates a certain urgency and imminence. Hopefully, the interrupter gets the message and lets you get back to work quickly.

6. Escort & Abandon

However, you may need to execute the Escort & Abandon maneuver if Stand & Stop doesn't work sufficiently. That is, if the interrupter doesn't get the message and launches into a story (etc.), pick up your coffee cup/water bottle and invite them to escort you to the breakroom. Once at the breakroom, fill up your cup/bottle, and abandon them by excusing yourself to get back to work!

We spend a lot of time at the office together. Pick one or two of these tactics to make the most of that time.

Productive Workspaces Exercise – Pick a Winner

Take a moment to consider these six suggestions. Put a check mark next to the one you are willing to try today.

- ☐ Create a Designated Workspace
- ☐ Sequester Yourself
- ☐ Partially Closed Door Trick
- ☐ Face Away from Traffic
- ☐ Stand & Stop
- ☐ Escort & Abandon

Consider the following questions when making your choice. Feel free to use the provided space to write out your answers.

1. Why do you like this tip?
2. How does it impact you positively?
3. What steps will you take to implement it

Answers to Questions:

Conclusion

The goal of this book is to find six minutes of productivity per day. Those six-minute increments aggregate into twenty-four additional hours of accomplishment per year. Select one or two of the suggestions made in this portion of the materials. Make a couple of small changes. A year from now, you'll be asking, *"What am I going to do with my three days, now that I have them?"*

Made in the USA
Middletown, DE
07 November 2018